This Book Belongs to:

KU-744-195

....

Consultant: Fiona Moss, RE Adviser at RE Today Services
Editor: Cathy Jones
Designer: Chris Fraser
Editorial Assistant: Tasha Percy
Managing Editor: Victoria Garrard
Design Manager: Anna Lubecka

Copyright © QED Publishing 2013

First published in the UK in 2013 by
QED Publishing
Part of The Quarto Group
The Old Brewery
6 Blundell Street
London N7 9BH

www.qed-publishing.co.uk

All rights reserved. No part of this publication may be reproduced,
stored in a retrieval system, or transmitted in any form or by any means,
electronic, mechanical, photocopying, recording, or
otherwise, without the prior permission of the publisher, nor be
otherwise circulated in any form of binding or cover other than
that in which it is published and without a similar condition
being imposed on the subsequent purchaser.

A catalogue record for this book is available
from the British Library.

ISBN 978 1 78171 175 0

Printed in China

The Miracles of Jesus

Written by
Katherine Sully

Illustrated by
Simona Sanfilippo

Jesus loved to teach God's message
and people loved to listen to him.

They followed him everywhere.

But one day, Jesus was sad because
his cousin, John, had died.
Jesus got on a boat
to rest and pray.

When he came back to shore, the people were still waiting for him.

Jesus welcomed them.

He started to teach and heal the sick people.

All day, Jesus spoke to the crowd.
When evening came, the disciples said to Jesus,
"It's late and these people are far from home.
Send them away, to buy some food."

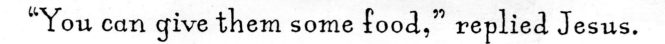

"You can give them some food," replied Jesus.

"That would cost too much!"
the disciples grumbled.

"Go and find out how much food we have,"
Jesus told his disciples.

The disciples went off
among the crowd. They came
back with a boy who had
five loaves and two fish.

Jesus told his disciples to sit everyone down in groups. Jesus took the five loaves and two fish and thanked God for the food.

Then he divided the food into baskets
for each of the disciples.

The disciples shared the
food among the people.

Everyone ate as much as they wanted.

CRUNCH!

MUNCH!

YUM!

After everyone had eaten, the disciples collected up the baskets.

When they came back, the twelve baskets were full of food!

They couldn't believe their eyes.

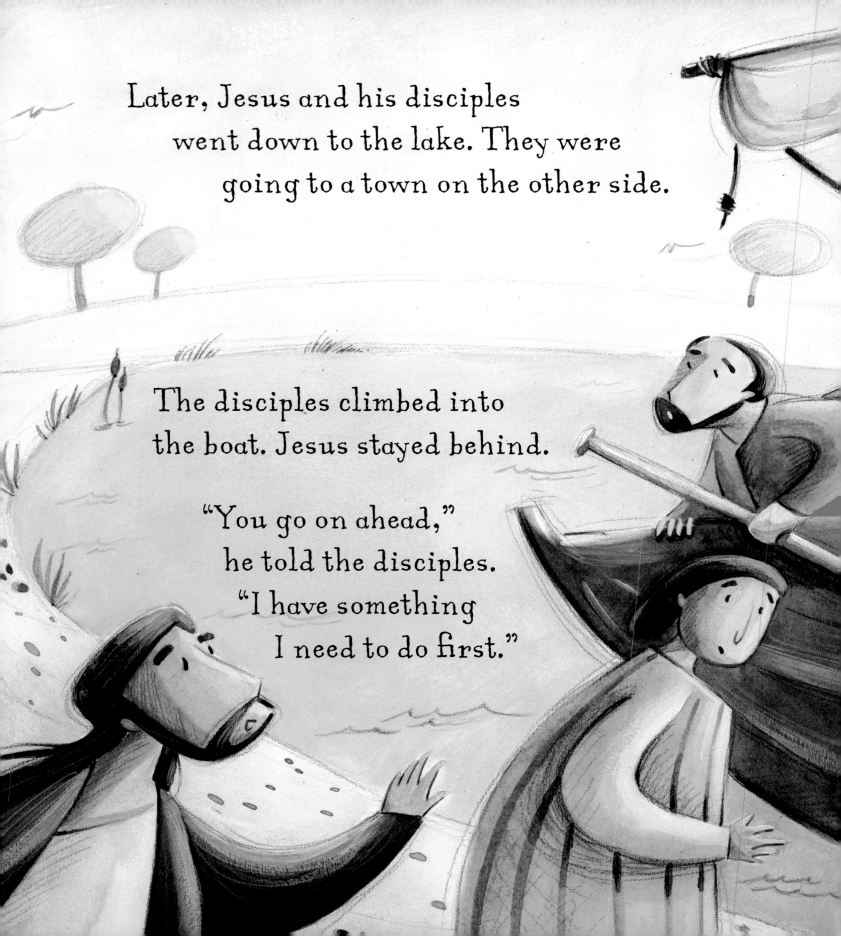

Later, Jesus and his disciples
went down to the lake. They were
going to a town on the other side.

The disciples climbed into
the boat. Jesus stayed behind.

"You go on ahead,"
he told the disciples.
"I have something
I need to do first."

At last, the crowd went home. Jesus sat alone
on the mountain to pray.

Later that night,
Jesus looked out
over the lake.

SPLASH!

CRASH!

The boat was now far from the shore,
tossing this way and that.
The disciples were struggling to row the boat,
fighting against the wind and the waves.

It was still dark when the disciples saw
a white figure coming towards them.
They were terrified.

"It's a ghost!" they cried.

But it was Jesus,
walking on the water.

Jesus called to the disciples,
"Be brave! It's only me!"

"Lord, if it's you," Peter replied,
"tell me to come to you on the water."

"Come," Jesus said.

So Peter got out of the boat and
walked on the water towards Jesus.
But he was scared and began to sink.

"Save me!" he cried.

Jesus reached out his hand and caught Peter.
"Did you doubt that God would save you?" Jesus asked.

As they climbed back into the boat,
the wind died down.
The disciples were amazed.

"You really are the Son of God,"
they said to Jesus.

Next Steps

Look back through the book to find more to talk about and join in with.

* Copy the actions. Do the actions with the characters – put your hands together to pray; row the boat; pretend you are sinking in the water like Peter.

* Join in with the rhyme. Pause to encourage joining in with
  "Five loaves and two fish.
  It's only enough to fill one dish!"

* Count in fives and twos. Count two fish, two oars, five loaves, five sheep.

* Name the colours. What colours are in the boy's hat? Look back to spot the colours on other pages.

* All shapes and sizes. Look for big, middle-size and small baskets and fish.

* Listen to the noisy crowd and storm. When you see the word on the page, point and make the sound – Crunch! Munch! Yum! Splash! Crash!

Now that you've read the story... what do you remember?

* Why was Jesus sad?
* How many people were in the crowd?
* What food did the disciples find?
* How many baskets of leftovers were there?
* Who walked on the water?
* How did people show they trusted God in the story?

What does the story tell us?
We should trust in God to give us all we need.